The Dhammapada

The Dhammapada
The path of the Dhamma

Astrolog Publishing House

Cover Design: Na'ama Yaffe

Production Manager: Dan Gold

P.O. Box 1123, Hod Hasharon 45111, Israel
Tel: 972-9-7412044
Fax: 972-97442714

© Astrolog Publishing House Ltd. 2005

ISBN 965-494-210-0

Published by Astrolog Publishing House 2005

The Dhammapada consists of 423 verses in Pali uttered by the Buddha on some 305 occasions for the benefit of a wide range of human beings. These sayings were selected and compiled into one book as being worthy of special note on account of their beauty and relevance for molding the lives of future generations of Buddhists. They are divided into 26 chapters and the stanzas are arranged according to subject matter.

Yammakavagga - The Pairs

(verses 1-20)

We are what we think.
The Mind is the master of our existence.
If one speaks or acts with a wicked mind,
he will bring suffering onto himself,
just as the wheel follows the ox
that pulls the cart.

We are what we think.
The Mind is the master of our existence.
If one speaks or acts with a pure mind,
he will attract joy and affection.
They will follow him like a shadow
that never leaves.

``He abused me,
he beat me,
he defeated me,
he robbed me,''

those who harbor such thoughts
will be filled with hatred.

``He abused me,
he beat me,
he defeated me,
he robbed me,''

those who do not harbor such thoughts
will know no hatred.

This is an eternal law.
Hate is not overcome by hate;
only Love, Metta, can conquer hate.
The others do not know
that in this quarrel we perish;
those of them who realize it,
can let go of their hate.

Whoever lives contemplating
the pleasures of life,
pleasing only the senses,
eating without moderation,
slothful and lethargic will be easily uprooted
like a weak tree in the wind.

Whoever lives contemplating ``the Impurities'',
with senses restrained,
eating with moderation,
full of faith,
full of sustained energy,
will stand strong in the wind,
like a rocky mountain.

The Dhammapada

He who lives in sin,
without self-control and truthfulness,
is not worthy of wearing the yellow robes.

He who lives a pure life,
is well-established in morals
and endowed with self-control
and truthfulness,
is indeed worthy of the yellow robe.

The one, who takes wrong to be right
and right to be wrong,
and who thinks always of sensual pleasures,
cannot be successful in finding the Truth.

The one, who takes right to be right
and wrong to be wrong,
and who thinks not of sensual pleasures,
can be successful in finding the Truth.

Like rain penetrates a poorly built house,
so does lust penetrate an undeveloped mind.
Like rain does not penetrate a strong house,
so does lust not penetrate
a well-developed mind.

The evildoer grieves both here
and in the afterlife.
He grieves perceiving
the impurity of his own deeds.

The honest man rejoices both here
and the afterlife.
In both states the he rejoices.
He rejoices, exceedingly rejoices,
perceiving the purity of his own deeds.

The evildoer suffers both here
and in the afterlife.
He suffers when he realizes
all the wrong he has done.
The honest man rejoices
both here and the afterlife.
He is happy to acknowledge
the good he has done.

Though much he recites the Sacred Texts
if he does not act accordingly,
a man has no share in the fruits of the Holy life.
Though little he recites the Sacred Texts,
but acts in accordingly with the teaching,
overcoming lust, hatred and ignorance
and living in truth, here and hereafter,
a man shares the fruits of the Holy life.

Appamadavagga - Heedfulness

(verses 21-32)

Fidelity is the path of the Deathless,
Nibbana, lack of it is the path to death.
Those who are careful and devoted
do not die;
the ignorant may as well be dead.

Distinctly understanding the difference,
the wise rejoice in their devotion,
delighting in the realm of Ariyas.

The constantly meditative,
the steadfast ones,
realize the supreme freedom,
Nibbana.

The man who is hard-working,
mindful, of pure conduct,
and careful,
who restrains himself,
who acts after due deliberations
and practices Right Livelihood,
becomes famous.

By sustained effort,
earnestness, discipline, and self-control,
let the wise man build himself an island,
which no flood overwhelms.

The unaware, foolish folk
indulge in their ignorance;
the wise man guards fidelity
as the greatest treasure.

Indulge not in ignorance;
have no intimacy with sensuous delights.
The meditative and devoted person
obtains abundant bliss.

When dedication and devotion
overpower a man's ignorance,
he becomes wise
and is free from sorrow.
He sees clearly the sorrowful
as one who stands on the hill
looking down on the plains.

Mindful among the careless,
watchful among the sleeping,
the wise man outstrips the foolish man
as a race horse outstrips an old horse.

Maghava, the king of gods,
attained such great supremacy

over the gods
through his fidelity.
Fidelity and attentiveness
are always praised
and ignorance is always blamed.

Even as a fire consumes all obstacles,
both great and small,
a monk, who delights in fidelity
and who views ignorance with fear,
consumes attachments,
both great and small.

A monk, who delights in fidelity
and who views ignorance with fear,
will not fail in the end to,
to attain Nibbana.

Cittavagga - The Mind

(verses 33-43)

The fickle, unsteady mind,
so hard to guard,
so hard to control,
the wise man straightens,
as the fletcher straightens the arrow.

Like a fish that is drawn from its watery
abode and thrown upon land,
this mind flutters attempting to shun
the realm of the passions.

The mind is hard to check.
It is swift and wanders at will.
To control it is good.
A controlled mind is conducive to happiness.

The mind is very hard to perceive,
extremely subtle and wanders at will.
Let the wise person guard it;
a guarded mind is conducive to happiness.

Faring far, wandering alone, bodiless,
lying in a cave, is the mind.
Those who subdue it are freed from
the bond of Mara.
He whose mind is not steadfast,
he who knows not true doctrine,
he whose confidence wavers –
his wisdom will never be perfect.

He whose mind is not consumed by lust,
he who has transcended both good and evil –
for such a vigilant one there is no fear.

Realizing that this body is as fragile as a jar,
establishing that this mind as firm as
a fortified city,
he should attack Mara
with the weapon of wisdom.
He should guard his conquest
and be without attachment.

Before long this body will lie upon the ground,
cast aside, devoid of consciousness,
even as a useless charred log.

Whatever harm a foe may do to a foe,
or a hater to a hater,
an ill-directed mind can do one
far greater harm.

What neither mother, nor father,
nor any other relative can do,
a well-directed mind does
and thereby elevates one.

Pupphavagga - Flowers

(verses 44-59)

Who will be able to understand himself,
this world, heaven and hell?
Who will fully realize
the well preached Doctrine,
which is like a garland fixed
by a clever garland maker?

The disciple in training, sekha,
will be able to understand himself,
this world, heaven and hell.
He will realize the well preached Doctrine,
which is like a garland
fixed by a clever garland maker.

Knowing that this body is like foam,
and comprehending its mirage-nature,
one should destroy the flowershafts
of sensual passions, Mara,
and pass beyond the sight
of the King of Death.

The man who gathers
the flowers of sensual pleasure,
whose mind is distracted,
death carries off as a great flood
sweeps away a sleeping village.
The man who gathers the flowers
of sensual pleasure,
whose mind is distracted,
and who is insatiate in desires,
the Destroyer brings
under his sway.

As a bee collects only the honey
without harming the flower,
its colors or scent,
so should the sage wander
in the village.

Not the faults of others,
nor what others have done
or left undone,
but one's own deeds,
done and left undone,
should one consider.

Like a beautiful and brilliant flower,
but without fragrance,
is the well-spoken but fruitless word
of one who does not practice it.

Like a beautiful and brilliant flower,
and full of fragrance too,
is the fruitful and well-spoken word
of one who does practice it.

Like many a garland is made
from a heap of flowers,
many a good deed
should be done by one born
as a human being.

The perfume of flowers blows
not against the wind,
nor does the fragrance
of sandalwood and jasmine,
but the fragrance of the virtuous
blows against the wind;
the virtuous man pervades every direction.

Sandalwood, lotus, jasmine:
above all these kinds of fragrance,
the perfume of virtue
is by far the best.

Of little account is the fragrance
of jasmine or sandalwood;
the fragrance of the virtuous,
which blows even amongst the gods,
is supreme.

Those, who are virtuous
and who live a life of devotion,
are set free by attaining perfect wisdom
and Mara cannot find a way to them.

The lotus will grow
even in rubbish thrown away.
It will delight the heart
with its sweet smell and beauty.

Just like a lotus,
the disciple, by his wisdom,
will shine among them
that are ignorant,
blind and unconverted.

Balavagga - *The Fool*

(verses 60-75)

Long is the night to the wakeful;
long is the league to the weary;
long is the samsara to the foolish
who know not the Sublime Truth.

If, as the disciple fares along,
he meets no companion who is better or equal,
let him firmly pursue his solitary career.
There is no fellowship with the foolish.

``Sons have I; wealth have I''
Such are the worries of the fool.
He himself is not his own.

The fool who knows that he is a fool
is for that very reason a wise man;
the fool who thinks that he is wise
is called a fool indeed.

Though a fool, through all his life,
associates with a wise man,

he no more understands the Dhamma
than a spoon tastes the flavor of soup.

Though an intelligent person
associates with a wise man
for only a moment,
he quickly understands the Dhamma
as the tongue tastes the flavor of soup.

Fools of little wit move about
with the very self as their own foe,
doing evil deeds that bear a bitter fruit.

It is a not a good deed when,
after having done it, one repents,
and when weeping, with tearful face,
one reaps the fruit thereof.

It is a good deed when,
after having done it,
one does not repent and when,
with joy and pleasure,
one reaps the fruit thereof.

An evil deed is as sweet as honey,
so thinks the fool.
As long as it does not ripen,
but when it ripens, then he grieves.
Month after month, a fool may eat
only as much food as can be picked up

on the tip of a blade of grass;
but he is not worth a sixteenth part
of them who have comprehended the Truth.

An evil deed committed
does not immediately bear fruit,
just as milk does not curdle at once;
smoldering, it follows the fool
like fire covered with ashes.

To his ruin, indeed,
the fool gains knowledge and fame;
they destroy his happiness
and cleave his head.

The fool will desire undue reputation,
precedence among monks,
authority in the monasteries,
honor among other families.

Let both laymen and monks think,
``by myself was this done; in everything,
great or small, let them refer to me''.
Such is the ambition of the fool;
his desires and pride increase.

Surely, the path that leads to worldly gain
is one,
and the path that leads to Nibbana
is another;

understanding this,
the Bhikkhu, the disciple of the Buddha,
should not rejoice in worldly favors,
but cultivate detachment.

Panditavagga - *The Wise Man*

(verses 76-89)

Should one see a wise man, who,
like a revealer of treasure,
points out faults and advises;
let one associate with such a wise person;
it will be better, not worse,
for him who associates with him.

Let him advise, instruct,
and dissuade one from evil;
truly pleasing is he to the good,
displeasing is he to the bad.

Associate not with evil friends,
associate not with mean men;
associate with good friends,
associate with noble men.

He who practices the Dhamma abides
in happiness with the mind pacified;
the wise man delights in the Dhamma
revealed by the Ariyas.

Irrigators lead the water;
fletchers fashion the shaft;
carpenters carve the wood;
the wise discipline themselves.

As a solid rock
is not shaken by the wind,
the wise remain unshaken
amidst blame and praise.

Just as a deep lake is clear and still,
the wise become exceedingly peaceful
upon hearing the teachings.

The good give up attachment;
the saintly do not blather about sensual craving;
whether affected by happiness or by pain,
the wise show neither elation nor depression.

A wise person does no wrong;
neither for the sake of oneself
nor for the sake of another.
He should not desire son, wealth, or kingdom
by doing wrong;
by unjust means he should not seek
his own success.
Only then is he indeed virtuous,
wise and righteous.

Few among men cross to the further shore.
The other folk only run up and down
the bank on this side.

But those who act rightly
accordingly to the teaching,
which is well expounded,
they will reach the Beyond-Nibbana,
the realm of passions,
so hard to cross.

A wise man renounces evil
and sensual pleasure
and he does all praiseworthy work
in order to attain Nibbana.
He becomes a homeless one.

By having no attachment and desires
and by forsaking sensual pleasures,
a wise man gets rid of his impurities.

Those, who practice the seven Factors:
Mindfulness, Investigation of the Dhamma,
Energy, Rapture, Calmness,
Concentration, and Equanimity,
and have freed themselves from attachments,
attain Nibbana.

Arahantavagga - *The Perfected One*

(verses 90-99)

For him who has completed the journey,
for him who knows not sorrow,
for him who from everything is wholly free,
for him who has destroyed all Ties,
the fever of passion does not exist.

The mindful exert themselves.
They are attached to no abode.
Like swans that leave their pools,
home after home they abandon.

Those who do not know greed
for worldly possessions,
who need nothing
and are nourished by wisdom alone -
their course like that of birds in the air -
cannot be traced.

He who has overcome corruption,
he who is not attached to food,
he who is free of worldly possessions
and nourished by wisdom -

his path, like that of birds in the air,
cannot be traced.

He whose senses are under his control,
like well-trained horses,
he whose pride is destroyed
and is free from corruption,
such a steadfast one even the gods hold dear.

An Arahant is not troubled with anything
just as the earth is not troubled with
clean and unclean things.
He is virtuous and pure,
as water free from mud.
He attains Nibbana.

Calm is his mind,
calm is his speech,
calm is his action,
who rightly knowing,
is wholly freed,
perfectly peaceful,
and balanced.

The man who is not naive,
who understands the Uncreate, Nibbana,
who has cut off the links,
who is unaffected by good and evil,
who has subdued all desires,
he indeed, is a supreme man.
Whether in village or in forest,

in gorge or on hill,
wherever Arahants dwell,
delightful, indeed, is that spot.

Delightful are the forests
where the ignorant are not found;
the passionless will rejoice
therefore they seek no sensual pleasures.

Sahassavagga - *The Thousands*

(verses 100-115)

A single beneficial word,
one that brings peace,
is better than a thousand
useless ones.

A single beneficial verse,
one that brings peace,
is better than a thousand verses,
comprising useless words.

One sentence of the Doctrine,
which brings happiness to a person
who understands it,
is better than one hundred stanzas
consisting of meaningless words.

Though one should conquer a thousand times
a thousand men in battle,
he who conquers his own self,
is the greatest of all conquerers.

Self-conquest is, indeed,
far greater than the conquest
of all other folks.

Neither a god nor a Gandhabba,
nor Mara with Brahma,
can win back the victory
of such a person
who is self-subdued
and ever lives in restraint.

Though month after month
with a thousand coins,
one should make an offering
for a hundred years,
if, only for a moment,
one should honor a Saint
who has perfected himself,
that honor is, indeed,
better than a century of sacrifice.

Though, for a century,
a man should tend
the sacred fire in the forest,
if, only for a moment,
he should honor a Saint
who has perfected himself,
that honor is, indeed,
better than a century of fire-sacrifice.

In this world whatever gift or alms
a person seeking merit
should offer for a year,
all that is not worth
a single quarter of the reverence
towards the Upright which is excellent.

For one who is in the habit
of constantly honoring and respecting
the elders,
four blessings increase -
age,
beauty,
bliss,
and strength.

Though one should live a thousand years,
immoral and uncontrolled,
yet better, indeed,
is a single day's life
of one who is moral and meditative.

Better, indeed, is a single day's life
of one who is wise and meditative
than a hundred years lived
without wisdom and control.

Better, indeed, is a single day's life
of one who makes an intense effort,
than a hundred years lived
idle and inactive.

Better, indeed, is a single day's life
of one who comprehends how all things
rise and pass away,
than a hundred years lived
without comprehending how all things
rise and pass away.

Better, indeed, is a single day's life
of one who sees the Deathless State than,
than a hundred years lived
without seeing the Deathless State.

Better, indeed, is a single day's life
of one who sees the Truth Sublime,
than a hundred years lived
not seeing the Truth Sublime..

Papavagga - *Evil*

(verses 116-128)

Make haste in doing good;
check your mind from evil;
for the mind of one who is slow
in doing good deeds
delights in evil.

Should a person commit evil,
he should not do it again and again;
he should not find pleasure therein:
painful is the accumulation of evil.

Should a person perform a good deed,
he should do it again and again;
he should find pleasure therein:
blissful is the accumulation of merit.

Even an evil-doer sees good,
as long as evil does not ripen;
but when it bears fruits,
then he sees the evil results.

Even a good person sees evil
so long as good does not ripen;
but when it bears fruits
then the good one sees the good results.

Do not disregard evil, saying,
``It will not come near me''.
By single drops even a water-jar is filled,
likewise the fool,
gathering little by little,
fills himself with evil.

Do not disregard merit, saying,
``It will not come near me'.;
By single drops even a water-jar is,
likewise the wise man,
gathering little by little,
fills himself with good.

Just as a merchant,
with a small escort and great wealth,
avoids a perilous route,
just as one desiring to live
avoids poison,
one should shun evil things.

If no wound there be in one's hand,
one may carry poison in it.
Poison does not affect one
who has no wound.
There is no ill for him who does no wrong.

The Dhammapada

Whoever harms a harmless person
who is pure and guiltless,
upon that very fool the evil recoils
like fine dust thrown against the wind.

Some are born in a womb;
evildoers are born in woeful states;
the well-conducted go to blissful states;
the Undefiled Ones pass away into Nibbana.

Not in the sky,
nor in the mid-ocean,
nor in a mountain cave,
is that place on earth
where abiding one may escape
from the consequences of one's evil deed.

Not in the sky,
nor in mid-ocean,
nor in a mountain cave,
is that place one earth
where abiding one will not be overcome
by death.

Dandavagga - *Violence*

(verses 129-145)

All tremble at violence.
All fear death.
Seeing ones' self in others,
one should neither strike
nor cause to strike.

All tremble at violence.
Life is dear to all.
Seeing ones' self in others,
one should neither strike
nor cause to strike.

Whoever tries to seek happiness
through hurting others,
cannot find happiness.

Whoever tries to seek happiness
without hurting others,
can find happiness.

Speak not harshly to anyone.
Those thus addressed will retort.

The Dhammapada

Painful, indeed, is vindictive speech.
Blows in exchange may bruise you.

If, like a cracked gong,
you silence yourself,
you have already attained Nibbana:
no vindictiveness will be found in you.

As with a staff the shepard
drives his cattle to pasture,
even so do old age and death
drive out the lives of beings.

So, when a fool does wrong deeds,
he does not realize their evil nature;
by his own deeds the stupid man
is tormented, like one burnt by fire.

Whosoever causes pain to the innocent ones
will himself suffer quickly from one
of the following ten states.

He will get sharp pain
or injury of the body,
or get serious illness
or become mad,
or punishment by the kind,
or being accused of doing wrong
or death of relatives
or loss of treasures,

or his house will be struck by lightning
or after death, he will be reborn in Hell.

Neither wandering naked,
nor matted locks,
nor filth,
nor fasting,
nor lying on the ground,
nor dust,
nor ashes,
nor striving squatting on the heels,
can purify a mortal
who has not overcome doubts.

Though elegant in attire,
if he should live in peace,
with passions subdued,
and senses controlled,
certain of the four Paths of Sainthood,
perfectly pure,
laying aside aggression in his relations
towards all living beings,
he is indeed a Brahmana,
an ascetic and a Bhikkhu.

Those, who are ashamed
to do shameful things,
are rare.
Such men can be compared
to a thoroughbred horse
who does not get whipped.

A man,
who practies virtue,
who has confidence in what he does,
who meditates
and who understands the Law,
such a man will get rid of suffering
as a thoroughbred horse
gets rid of being whipped.

Irrigators lead the waters.
Fletchers bend the shafts.
Carpenters fashion the wood.
The virtuous control themselves.

Jaravagga - *Old Age*

(verses 146-156)

What is laughter, what is joy,
when the world is ever burning?
Shrouded by darkness,
would you not seek the light?

Behold this beautiful body,
a mass of sores, a heaped-up lump,
diseased, much thought of,
in which nothing lasts, nothing persists.

Thoroughly worn out is this body,
a nest of diseases, perishable.
This putrid mass breaks up.
Truly, life ends in death.

Life gourds cast away in autumn
are these weak bones.
What pleasure is there
in looking at them?

The city which you are is made of bones,
plastered with flesh and blood.

The Dhammapada

Herein are stored decay,
death, conceit, and detraction.

Even ornamented royal chariots wear out.
So too the body reaches old age.
But the Dhamma of the Good
does not grow old.
The Good reveal it among the Good.

The man of little learning
grows old like the ox.
His muscles grow;
his wisdom does not grow.

I wandered years, seeking,
but not finding,
the builder of this house
that is my self.
It is sorrowful to be born
again and again.

O house-builder! I have seen you.
You shall build no house again.
All the rafters are broken.
Thy ridge-pole is shattered.
My mind has attained the unconditioned.
The end of craving is achieved.

They who have not led the Holy Life,
who in youth had not acquired wealth,

pine away like old herons
at a pond without fish.

They who have not led the Holy Life,
who in youth had not acquired wealth,
like worn out bows sigh
after the past.

Attavagga - *The Self*

(verses 157-166)

If one holds oneself dear,
one should protect oneself well.
During every one of the three watches
the wise man should keep vigil.

Let one first establish oneself
in what is proper,
and then instruct others.
Such a wise man will not be tainted.

One should practice what he preaches.
Only when fully controlled,
he should control others;
for oneself, indeed,
is difficult to control.

One own self, indeed,
is one's savior,
for what other savior would there be?
With oneself well controlled
one obtains a savior difficult to find.

By oneself alone is evil done;
it is self-born, it is self-caused.
Evil grinds the unwise
as a diamond grinds a hard gem.

Just as the vine covers the tree
and destroys it,
the man who allows
his wickedness to overcome him,
suffers as much as his enemy
would have him suffer.

Easy to do are things
that are not beneficial to oneself,
but very, very difficult, indeed,
to do is that which is beneficial and good.

Whosoever rejects the words
of the noble, righteous Arahants,
such a fool,
because of his false views,
brings forth on his head
ruin and destruction,
like the banana-tree which dies
when it has borne fruit.

By oneself, indeed, is evil done;
by oneself is one tainted.
By oneself is evil left undone;
by oneself, indeed, is one purified.

The Dhammapada

Purity and impurity depend on oneself.
No one purifies another.

For the sake of others' welfare,
however great,
let not one neglect one's own welfare.
Clearly perceiving one's own welfare
let one be intent on one's own goal.

Lokavagga - *The World*

(verses 167-178)

Do not follow a life of evil;
do not live carelessly;
do not have false views;
do not value worldly things.
In this way one can get rid of suffering.

A man should not live carelessly
but should exert himself to live righteously.
Such a man is happy
in this world
and in the next.

A man should live righteously
and not wrongly.
Such a man is happy in this world
and in the next.

Just as one would look upon a bubble,
just as one would look upon a mirage -
if a person thus looks upon the world,
the King of Death does not see him.

Come, behold this world
which is like unto
an ornamented royal chariot,
filled with misguided fools,
but for the wise there is no attachment.

A man, who is free from heedlessness
and is heedless no more,
purifies himself and shines in this world
like the moon which is freed from a cloud.

Whosoever, by a good deed,
corrects the evil done,
illuminates this world like the moon
freed from clouds.

Blind is this world.
Few are those who clearly see.
As birds escape from a net,
few go to a blissful state.

As swans can fly easily through the air,
as those who persevere
can perform wonders,
wise men can easily conquer death.

There is no evil that cannot be done by the liar,
who has transgressed the one law of truthfulness
and who is indifferent to a world beyond.

Misers do not go to the celestial realms.
Fools do not indeed praise kindness.
The wise man rejoices in giving
and thereby becomes happy thereafter.

Better than absolute sovereignity over the earth,
better than lordship over all the worlds
is the joy of liberation,
being one with the flow of life.

Buddhavagga - *The Buddha*

(verses 179-196)

One who has conquered all defilements,
cannot be defeated.
He is The Buddha,
who has attained unlimited power.

One, who has no Craving
with its snare and poisons,
cannot be disturbed.
He is The Buddha,
who has attained unlimited power.

The wise ones who are intent on meditation,
who delight in the peace
of renunciation, Nibbana,
such mindful perfect Buddhas
even the gods hold dear.

Rare is birth as a human being.
Hard is the life of mortals.
Hard it is to obtain the chance
to listen to the Dhamma.
Rare is the appearance of the Buddhas.

To cease from all evil,
to cultivate good,
to purify one's mind:
This is the advice of all Buddhas.

Patience is the highest importance,
say the Buddhas.
He, who is patient,
is not a recluse who harms another.
Nor is he an ascetic who oppresses others.

Not insulting, not harming, restraint
according to the Fundamental Moral Code,
moderation in food, secluded dwelling,
intent on higher thoughts,
this is the Teaching of the Buddhas.

One who craves,
cannot be satisfied
even when he has
plenty of gold.
The wise man does not crave
as he understands
the consequences of craving.

A wise man finds no delight
in heavenly pleasures.
The disciple of The Buddha
takes delight in the destruction of Craving.

Fearful men find many a refuge,
hills, woods, groves, trees, and shrines.

No such refuge is safe,
no such refuge is supreme.
Not by resorting to such a refuge
is one freed from all ill.

He who has to the Buddha,
the Dhamma,
and the Sangha for refuge,
sees the Four Noble Truths -
Sorrow,
the Cause of Sorrow,
the Transcending of Sorrow
and the Noble Eightfold Path
which leads to the Cessation of Sorrow.

This, indeed, is a secure refuge.
This, indeed, is a secure refuge .
By seeking such a refuge
is one released from all sorrow.

A man of great wisdom is hard to find:
such a man is not born everywhere.
Where such a wise man is born,
that family lives happily.

Happy is the birth of Buddhas.
Happy is the teaching of the sublime Dhamma.

Happy is the unity of Sangha.
Happy is the discipline of the united one.

He who honors those worthy of honor,
he who has overcome all passions,
he has overcome Suffering,
he has gained great merit.

Sukhavagga - *Happiness*

(verses 197-208)

*Ah, happily do we live
without hate amongst the hateful;
amidst hateful men
we dwell without hatered.*

*Ah, happily do we live
in good health amongst the ailing;
amidst ailing men
we dwell in good health
free from the disease of passions.*

*Ah, happily do we live
without yearning for sensual pleasures
amongst those who yearn for them;
amidst those who yearn
we dwell without yearning.*

*Ah, happily do we live,
we who have no impediments.
We shall be Feeders of joy
like the gods of the Radiant Realm.*

Victory breeds hatred.
The defeated live in pain.
Happily the peaceful live,
giving up victory and defeat.

There is no fire like lust,
no crime like hate.
There is no ill like the body,
no bliss higher than Peace, Nibbana.

Hunger is the greatest disease.
Excess is the greatest ill.
Knowing this as it really is,
the wise realize Nibbana's, supreme bliss.

Good health is the highest gain.
Contentment is the greatest wealth.
Trustworthy ones are the best kinsmen.
Nibbana is the highest Bliss.

Having tasted the flavor of seclusion
and the flavor of appeasement,
free from anguish and stain he becomes,
imbibing the taste of the joy of the Dhamma.

Happy is one who beholds the holy ones.
To live with the holy ones is ever pleasant.
It would be pleasant if one never comes
across a fool.

Truly, he who moves in company with fools
grieves for a long time.
Association with the foolish
is ever painful as with a foe.
Happy is association with the wise,
like meeting with family.

Therefore -
With the intelligent,
the wise,
the learned,
the enduring,
the dutiful
and the Ariya -
with a man of such virtue and intellect
should one associate,
just as the moon follows the starry path.

Piyavagga - *Affection*

(verses 209-220)

*Applying oneself to that
which should be avoided,
not applying oneself to that
which should be pursued,
and giving up the quest,
one who goes after pleasure
envies them who exert themselves.*

*Do not socialize much
with those that are dear,
never with those that are not dear;
not seeing those that are dear
and seeing those that are not dear,
are both painful.*

*Hence hold nothing dear,
for separation from those
that are dear is painful;
bonds do not exist for those
to whom nothing is dear or not dear.*

From endearment springs grief,
from endearment springs fear;
for him who is wholly free from endearment
there is no grief or fear.

From affection arises grief;
from affection arises fear;
for him who is free from affection
there is no grief or fear.

From attachment springs grief,
from attachment springs fear;
for him who is wholly free from attachment
there is no grief or fear.

From lust arises grief,
from lust arises fear;
for him who is free from lust
there is no grief or fear.

From craving arises grief,
from craving arises fear;
for him who is free from craving
there is no grief or fear.

The one who is perfect in virtue and insight,
is established in the Dhamma,
has realized the Truths,
and fulfils his own duties,
he is the one folks hold dear.

He who has developed a wish
for the Undeclared Nibbana,
he whose mind is thrilled
with the three Fruits,
he whose mind is not bound
by material pleasures,
such person is called
an ``Upstream-bound One''.

A man long absent and returned safe
from afar, his family, friends, and well-wishers
welcome him on his arrival.

Likewise, his good deeds will receive
the well-doer who has done
from this world to the next,
as family will receive a dear one on his return.

Kodhavagga - *Anger*

(verses 221-234)

Put anger away, abandon pride,
overcome every attachment,
cling not to Mind and Body
and thus be free from sorrow.

One,
who controls his anger when aroused,
is like a clever driver
who controls a fast going carriage;
the others
are like those who merely hold the reins.

Conquer the angry man by love;
conquer the ill-natured man by goodness;
conquer the miser with generosity;
conquer the liar with truth.

One should speak the truth,
and not yield to anger;
when asked one should give
though there be litter;

The path of the Dhamma   **65**

by these three things one may go
to the presence of the devas, the gods.

Those sages who are harmless,
and are ever restrained in body,
go to the deathless state, Nibbana,
although they are gone they never grieve.

The flaws of those who are ever vigilant,
who discipline themselves day and night,
who are wholly intent on Nibbana,
are destroyed.

This is a thing of old, Atula, not only of today;
they blame him who remains silent,
they blame him who talks much,
they blame him who speaks in moderation;
no one in the world is left unblamed.

There never was, there never will be,
nor is there now to be found anyone
who is always blamed or always praised.

Examining day by day, the wise
praise him who leads a flawless life,
intelligent, endowed with knowledge and virtue.

Who dares to blame him who
is like a piece of refined gold?
Even the gods praise him;
by Brahma too he is praised.

One should guard against misdeeds
caused by the body,
and one should be restrained in body.
Giving up evil conduct in body,
one should be of good bodily conduct.

One should guard against misdeeds
caused by speech,
and one should be restrained in speech.
Giving up the evil conduct in speech,
one should be one good conduct in speech.

One should guard against misdeeds
caused by the mind,
and one should be restrained in mind.
Giving up evil conduct in mind,
one should be of good conduct in mind.

The wise are restrained in deed;
in speech, too, they are restrained.
The wise, restrained in mind,
are indeed those who are perfectly restrained.

Malavagga - *Impurity*

(verses 235-255)

Like a withered leaf are you now.
The messengers of death wait on you.
On the threshold of decay you stand.
Yet, you have no provision for your journey.

Make an island unto yourself.
Strive quickly; become wise.
Without strain and passionless,
you shall enter the heavenly stage of the Ariyas.

Your life has come to end now.
To the presence of death you are setting out.
There is nowhere for you to stop along the way.
There is no provision for you either.

Make an island unto yourself.
Strive without delay; become wise.
Without strain and passionless,
you will not come again to birth and old age.

The Dhammapada

By degrees,
little by little,
from time to time,
a wise person should remove
his own impurities,
like a silversmith polishes silver.

As rust sprung from iron
eats itself away when arisen,
his own deeds lead the transgressor
to states of woe.

Texts not repeated are often soon forgotten;
the house neglected soon decays;
sloth is a blemish on beauty;
heedlessness is a blemish on the watchman.

Misconduct is the taint of a woman.
Stinginess is the taint of a donor.
Taints, indeed, are all evil things
both in this world and in the next.

A worse taint than these is ignorance,
the greatest taint.
Abandoning this taint,
be taintless, O Bhikkhus!

Easy is the life of a man who is shameless,
bold like a crow, a fault finder, insolent,
impudent and corrupt.

Hard is the life of one who is modest,
who ever seeks purity, is detached,
humble, clean in life and reflective.

One who destroys life,
utters lies,
takes what is not given,
resorts to others' wife,
and is addicted to intoxicating liquor,
he, in this very life,
would dig up his own root.

Know thus, O good man:
``not easy to control are evil things''.
Let not greed and hate drag you
to suffering for a long period.

People give according
to their faith and pleasure.
Whoever allows himself to be annoyed
because of the good deeds of others,
such a man cannot get peace of mind
by day or by night.

But he who has fully cut off this feeling,
uprooted and destroyed,
gains peace
by day and by night.

There is no fire like lust,
no grip like hate,

no net like delusions,
no river like craving.

Easily seen are others' faults,
hard indeed to see are one's own.
Like banter one speaks of others' faults,
but one hides his own faults one,
like a crafty fowler
conceals himself by camouflage.

He who sees others' faults,
and is ever irritable -
his corruptions grow.
He is far from the destruction of corruptions.

In the sky there is no track.
Outside there is no Saint.
Mankind delights in obstacles.
The Tathagatas are free from obstacles.

In the sky there is no track.
Outside there is no Saint.
There are no conditioned things that are eternal.
There is no instability in the Buddhas.

Dhammatthavagga - *The Just*

(verses 256-272)

He who is not just, arbitrates hastily.
He, who inquires into what is right and wrong,
is indeed just and wise.

The intelligent person
who does not lead others falsely
but lawfully and impartially,
who is a guardian of the law, is called
``one who abides by the law'',
dhammamattha.

He who speaks much is not called wise.
He, who is patient, thoughtful,
free from hatred and fear,
he is indeed called a wise man.

He, who speaks much is not
the one well versed in the Law.
He, who hears the Law and practices
what he has learned
is the one who knows the Law.

He is not thereby an Elder
merely because his head is grey.
Ripe is his age.
``Old-in-vain'' is he called.

The one in whom are truth, virtue,
harmlessness, restraint and control,
that wise man who is purged of impurities,
is, indeed, called an Elder.

A man, even if he is fair in complexion
or good in speech,
will never be accomplished,
if he is greedy, envious and deceitful.

But a man in whom these are wholly cut off,
uprooted and extinct,
that wise man who is purged of hatred,
is, indeed, called good-natured.

Not by a shaven head
does an undisciplined man,
who utters lies,
become a monk.
How will one who is full of desire and greed
be a monk?

He who completely subdues evil deeds
both small and great,
is called a monk
because he has overcome all evil.

The path of the Dhamma   **73**

He is not thereby a Bhikkhu
merely because he seeks alms from others;
by following the whole code of morality
one certainly becomes a Bhikkhu
and not merely by seeking alms.

A man who has transcended
both good and evil,
whose conduct is sublime,
who lives with understanding in this world,
he, indeed, is called a Bhikkhu.

Not by silence alone does one
who is dull and ignorant
become a sage;
but that wise man,
who as if holding a pair of scales,
embraces the best and shuns evil,
is indeed a sage.

For that reason embracing the best
and abandoning evil
he is a sage.
He who understands both worlds is, therefore,
called a sage.

He is not therefore an Ariya, Noble,
if he harms living beings;
through his harmlessness towards all living beings
is he called an Ariya, Noble.

The Dhammapada

Not only by mere morality and austerities
nor again by much learning,
nor even by developing mental concentration,
nor by secluded lodging, thinking,
``I enjoy the bliss of renunciation
not resorted to by the worldling"
should you, O Bhikkhu,
rest content without reaching the extinction
of the corruptions, Arahatship.

Maggavagga - *The Path*

(verses 273-289)

The best of all paths is the Eightfold Path.
The best of all truths are the Four Noble Truths.
Non-attachment is the best of all states.
The best of all men is the Seeing One,
the Buddha.

This is the only Way.
There is none other for the purity of vision.
Follow this path.
Overcome your desires, Mara.

Entering upon that path you will find
the end of pain.
By teaching you the removal of thorns,
I have taught you the path.

Striving should be done by alone;
the Tathagatas are only teachers.
The meditative ones who enter the way
are delivered from the bonds of Mara.

``Transient are all conditioned things'':
when one discerns this, with wisdom,
then is one is disgusted with ill;
this is the path to purity.

``Sorrowful are all conditioned things'':
when when one discerns this, with wisdom,
then is one is disgusted with ill;
this is the path to purity.

``All Dhammas are without a soul'':
when this, with wisdom, one discerns,
then is one is disgusted with ill;
this is the path to purity.

Who does not strives when it is time to strive,
who though young and strong is apathetic,
who is low in mind and thought and lazy,
that idler never finds the way to wisdom.

Watchful of speech,
and well controlled in mind,
let him do no evil with the body;
let him purify these three ways of action
and attain the path attained by the Sages.

Surely, from meditation arises wisdom.
Without meditation wisdom wanes.
Knowing this twofold path of gain and loss,
let one so conduct oneself
that wisdom may increase.

Cut down the forest of passions,
but not real trees.
From the forest of passions springs fear.
Cut down both forest
and brush wood of passions,
be forestless, O Bhikkhus.

For as long as the slightest brushwood
of passions of man towards women
is not cut down,
so long is his mind in bondage,
like the calf to its mother-cow.

Cut off your affection
as though it were an autumn lily,
with the hand.
Cultivate the very path of peace.
Nibbana has been expounded
by the Auspicious One.

Here will I live in the rainy season,
here in the autumn and in the summer:
thus muses the fool.
He does not realize the danger of death.

The doting man with mind set
on children and herds,
death seizes and carries away,
as a great flood sweeps away
a slumbering village.

There are no sons for one's protection,
neither father nor even family;
for one who is overcome by death,
no protection is to be found among family.

Realizing this fact,
let the virtuous and wise person swiftly
clear the way that leads to Nibbana.

Pakinnakavagga - *Miscellaneous*

(verses 290-305)

If by giving up a lesser happiness,
one may behold a greater one,
let the wise man give up the lesser happiness
in consideration of the greater happiness.

He who wishes his own happiness
by causing pain to others
is not released from hatred,
being himself entangled
in the tangles of hatred.

What should have been done is left undone,
what should not have been done is done.
Because of those who are
puffed up and arrogant
the corruptions increase.

Those who always earnestly practice
``mindfulness of the body'',
who follow not what should not be done,
and constantly do what should be done,

*Because of those mindful and reflective ones
the corruptions come to an end.*

*Having slain mother, craving, and father, conceit,
and two warrior kings whose views are based on
eternalism and nihilism, and having destroyed a
country together with its revenue officer, attachment,
ungrieving goes the Brahmana (Arahant).*

*Having slain mother and father and two brahmin kings,
and having destroyed the perilous path (hindrances),
ungrieving goes the Brahmana (Arahant).*

*Well awakened
the disciples of Gotama arise -
they who by day and night
always contemplate the Buddha.*

*Well awakened
the disciples of Gotama arise -
they who by day and night
always contemplate the Dhamma.*

*Well awakened
the disciples of Gotama ever -
they who by day and night
always contemplate the Sangha.*

*Well awakened
the disciples of Gotama arise -*

they who by day and night
always contemplate the body.

Well awakened
the disciples of Gotama ever -
they who by day and night
always delight in harmlessness.

Well awakened
the disciples of Gotama arise -
they who by day and night
always delight in meditation.

Difficult in renunciation,
difficult to delight therein.
Difficult and painful is household life.
Painful is association with those
who are incompatible.
Ill befalls a wanderer in samsara.
Therefore be not a wanderer
be not a pursuer of ill.

He who is full of confidence and virtue,
possessed of fame and wealth,
is honored everywhere,
in whatever land he sojourns.

Even from afar like the Himalaya's
the good reveal themselves.
The wicked, though near,
are invisible like arrows shot by night.

He, who sits alone,
rests alone,
walks alone and aware,
who in solitude controls himself,
will find delight in the forest.

Nirayavagga - *The State of Woe*

(verses 306-319)

The liar goes to a woeful state,
and also he who,
having done wrong,
says, ``I did not.''
Both after death become equal,
in the other world.

Those who put on the yellow robes,
who do evil
and who are uncontrolled in their passions,
they will go to hell
because of their evil.

Better to swallow a red-hot iron ball,
which would consume one
like a flame of fire,
than to be an immoral and uncontrolled person
feeding on the alms offered by people.

Four misfortunes befall a heedless man
who commits adultery:

acquisition of demerit,
disturbed sleep,
blame,
and a state of woe.

There is acquisition of demerit
as well as evil destiny.
Brief is the joy of the frightened
man and woman.
The King imposes a heavy punishment.
Hence no man should frequent another's wife.

Just as Kusa grass,
wrongly grasped,
cuts the hands,
even so the monkhood wrongly handled drags
one to a woeful state.

Any loose act,
any corrupt practice,
a life of dubious holiness -
none of these is of much fruit.

If it should be done,
let one do it.
Let one promote it steadily,
for slack asceticism scatters dust all the more.

An evil deed is better not done:
a misdeed torments one hereafter.

Better it is to do a good deed,
which after doing, one does not grieve.

Guard yourself like a border city,
guarded within and without.
Do not let slip this opportunity,
for they who let slip the opportunity
grieve when born in a sorrowful state.

Those who feel shame when they ought not to,
and do not feel shame when they ought to,
such men due to their wrong views
go to sorrowful states.

Those who are afraid
when there should be no fear,
and are not afraid
when there should be fear,
such men, due to their wrong views
go to sorrowful states.

Those who see faults in the faultless,
and perceive no wrong in that which is wrong,
such men, due to their wrong views
go to sorrowful states.

Those who know wrong as wrong
and right as right,
such men, due to their right views
go to a blissful state.

The Dhammapada

Nagavagga - *The Elephant*

(verses 320-333)

Like an elephant in the battlefield
withstands the arrows shot from a bow,
I will endure abuse;
indeed most people are undisciplined.

They lead the trained horses or elephants
to an assembly.
The king mounts the trained animal.
Best among men are the trained
who endure abuse.

Excellent are trained mules,
so are thorough-bred horses of Sindh
and noble tusked elephants;
but far better is he who has trained himself.

Surely never by those vehicles
would one go to the unknown land, Nibbana,
as does one who is controlled
through his subdued and well-trained self.

The elephant is not satisfied
with the food in luxurious places.
It longs to go back to the jungle
among its relations.

The man who is lazy and a glutton,
who eats large meals and rolls in his sleep
like a pig which is fed in the sty
is reborn again and again.

Formerly this mind wandered about
where it liked, wherever it willed, as it pleased;
today, with wisdom and meditation
I shall control it as a mahout controls
an elephant in rut.

Take delight in heedfulness.
Guard your mind well.
Draw yourselves out of the evil way
just as the elephant sunk in the mud
draws himself out.

Should one find a good companion to walk with
and who is steadfast and upright,
one should walk with him
with joy so as to overcome all dangers.

If no such companion is found;
it is better to travel alone
like a king who has left his kingdom,

or an elephant
which has left its companions.

It is better to live alone;
there is no fellowship with a fool.
Let one live alone committing no evil,
being carefree,
like a Matanga elephant roaming at will
in the forest.

When need arises,
it is pleasant to have friends.
It is pleasant to be content with just this and that.
Pleasant is merit when life is at an end.
Pleasant is the shunning of all ill.

Pleasant in this world is mothering.
Fathering, too, is pleasant in this world.
It is pleasant to strive for a pure and noble life.

Pleasant is virtue continued until old age.
Pleasant is steadfast confidence.
Pleasant is the attainment of wisdom.
Pleasant is it to do no evil.

Tanhavagga - *Craving*

(verses 334-359)

The craving of the heedless man
grows like a Maluva, an all entangling vine.
He runs hither and thitherfrom one life to another
like a monkey in the forest looking for fruit.

Whosoever in this world is overcome
by this base craving,
this clinging to objects,
his sorrows grow like Birana grass after rain.

Whosoever in this world overcomes
this base craving so hard to subdue,
his sorrows fall away from him
like water drops from a lotus leaf.

This I say to you all who have assemblid here:
Dig up the root of craving like one in quest
of Birana's sweet root.
Let not Mara crush you again and again
as a flood crushes a reed.

Like a tree cut down begins to grow up again
if its roots remain uninjured and firm,
when the root of craving remain undestroyed,
this suffering arises again and again.

A man who gives way to pleasure
will be swept away by craving
and his thoughts will make him suffer,
like waves.

The streams of craving flow everywhere.
The creeper, craving, sprouts and stands.
Seeing the vine that has grown,
cut off the roots with wisdom.

A man's joys are always transient,
and since men devote themselves to pleasure,
seeking after happiness,
they undergo birth and decay.

Folks engulfed in craving
are terrified like a captive hare.
Held fast by fetters and bonds,
they come to sorrow again and again.

Folks engulfed in craving
are terrified like a captive hare.
Therefore a Bhikkhu who wishes to be passionless,
Nibbana, should discard craving.

One with no desire for the household
finds pleasure in the forest of simplicity and,
though freed from desire
runs back to that very home.
Come, behold that man!
Freed, he runs back into that very bondage.

That which is made of iron, wood or hemp,
is not a strong bond, say the wise;
the longing for jewels, ornaments,
children, and wives
is a far greater attachment.

That bond is strong, say the wise.
It hurls down, is supple, and is hard to loosen.
This too the wise cut off,
and leave the world, with no longing,
renouncing sensual pleasures.

Those who are infatuated with lust
fall back into the stream
like a spider into the web it has spun itself.
This too the wise cut off and wander,
with no longing, released from all sorrow.

Let the past go.
Let the future go.
Let the present, front, back and middle go.
Crossing to the farther shore of existence,
with the mind released from everything,
do not again undergo birth and decay.

For the person who is disturbed by evil thoughts,
who is exceedingly lustful,
who contemplates pleasant things,
craving increases more and more.
Surely he makes the bond of Mara stronger.

He who delights in subduing evil thoughts,
who meditates on ``the loathsomeness'' of the body,
who is ever mindful,
it is he who will achieve an end of craving.
He will sever Mara's bond.

He who has reached the goal,
is fearless,
is without craving,
is passionless,
has cut off the thorns of life.
This is his final body.

He who is without craving and grasping,
who is skilled in etymology and terms,
who knows the grouping of letters
and their sequence,
it is he who is called the bearer of the final body,
one of profound wisdom,
a great man.

All have I overcome,
all do I know.
I am detached from all.

The path of the Dhamma

I have renounced all.
Wholly absorbed am I in
``the destruction of craving''.
Having comprehended all by myself,
whom shall I call my teacher?

The gift of Truth excels all other gifts.
The flavor of Truth excels all other flavors.
The pleasure in Truth excels all other pleasures.
He who has destroyed craving
overcomes all sorrow.

Riches ruin the foolish,
but not those in quest of the Beyond, Nibbana.
Through craving for riches
the ignorant man ruins himself
as well as others.

Weeds are the bane of the fields,
lust is the bane of mankind.
Hence what is given to those
who do not lust yields abundant fruit.

Weeds are the bane of the fields,
hatred is the bane of mankind.
Hence what is given to those rid of hatred
yields abundant fruit.

Weeds are the bane of the fields,
delusion is the bane of mankind.

Hence what is given to those rid of delusion
yields abundant fruit.

Weeds are the bane of fields,
craving is the bane of mankind.
Hence what is given to those rid of craving
yields abundant fruit.

Bhikkhuvagga - *The Monk*

(verses 360-382)

Good is restraint of the eye;
good is restraint of the ear;
good is restraint of the nose;
good is the restraint of the tongue.

Good is restraint in deed;
good is restraint in speech;
good is restraint in mind;
good is restraint in everything.
The Bhikkhu, restrained at all points,
is freed from sorrow.

He who is controlled in hand,
in foot, in speech, and in the highest, the head;
he who delights in meditation, and is composed;
he who is alone, and is contented,
him they call a Bhikkhu.

The Bhikkhu who is controlled in tongue,
who speaks wisely,
who is not puffed up,

who explains the meaning and the text,
sweet, indeed, is his speech.

That Bhikkhu who dwells in the Dhamma,
who delights in the Dhamma,
who meditates on the Dhamma,
who well remembers the Dhamma,
does not fall away
from the sublime Dhamma.

Let him not despise what he has received,
nor should he live envying the gains of others.
The Bhikkhu who envies the gains of others
does not attain concentration.

Though receiving but little,
if a Bhikkhu does not despise his own gains,
even the gods praise such a one
who is pure in livelihood and is not slothful.

He who has no thought
of ``I'' and ``mine''
whatever towards mind and body,
he who does not grieve
for that which he has not, he is, indeed,
called a Bhikkhu.

The Bhikkhu who abides in loving-kindness,
who is pleased with the Buddha's Teaching,
attains that state of peace and happiness,
the stilling of conditioned things.

Empty this boat, O Bhikkhu!
Emptied by you it will move swiftly.
Cutting off lust and hatred,
to Nibbana you will thereby go.

Cut off the five fetters pertaining to this shore self-
illusion, doubt, indulgence in wrongful rites and
ceremonies, sense-desires and hatred, throw off the
five fetters that pertain to the Further Shore, attachment
to the realm of form, attachment to formless realms,
conceit, restlessness and ignorance, cultivate further
five faculties confidence, energy, mindfulness,
concentration and wisdom. He who has destroyed
the five fetters lust, hatred, delusion, pride and false
views is called a ``Flood Crosser''.

Monks, meditate!
Do not be careless,
do not pursue the pleasure of sense
to sway your heart
lest passions will toss you about
and you will suffer.

There is no concentration in one
who lacks wisdom,
nor is there wisdom in him
who lacks concentration.
One who has both concentration and wisdom,
he, indeed, is in the presence of Nibbana.

The Bhikkhu who has retired
to a lonely abode,
who has calmed his mind,
who perceives the doctrine clearly,
experiences a joy transcending that of men.

Whenever he reflects on the rise and fall
of the Aggregates,
he experiences joy and happiness.
To ``those who know''
that reflection is Deathless.

And this becomes the beginning here
for a wise Bhikkhu:
sense-control, contentment, restraint
with regard to the Fundamental Code, patimokkha,
association with benevolent and energetic friends
whose livelihood is pure.

Let him be cordial in his ways
and refined in conduct;
filled thereby with joy he will
achieve an end of ill.

Like the jasmine sheds its withered flowers, Bhikkhu,
you should totally cast off lust and hatred.

The Bhikkhu who is calm in body,
calm in speech,
calm in mind,

who is well-composed,
who has spewed out worldly things
is truly called a ``peaceful one''.

You reprimand yourself.
You examine yourself.
Self-guarded and mindful, O Bhikkhu,
you will live happily.

Self, indeed, is the protector of self.
Self, indeed, is one's refuge.
Therefore, control your own self
like a merchant controls a noble stallion.

Full of joy, full of confidence
in the Buddha's Teaching,
the Bhikkhu will attain the Peaceful State,
the stilling of conditioned things,
the supreme bliss.

The Bhikkhu who,
while still young,
devotes himself to the Buddha's Teaching,
illuminates this world like the moon
freed from a cloud.

Brahmanavagga - *The Holy Man*

(verses 383-423)

Strive and cut off the stream of craving.
Discard, O Brahmana, sensual desires.
Knowing the destruction of conditioned things,
be, O Brahmana,
a knower of the Unmade, Nibbana.

When in two states insight and concentration,
a Brahmana goes to the Farther Shore,
then all the fetters of that ``one who knows''
pass away.

The one for whom there exists neither
the near nor the farther shore,
nor both the hither and the farther shore,
he who is undistressed and unbound,
him I call a Brahmana.

He who is meditative, stainless and secluded,
he who has done his duty
and is free from corruptions,
he who has attained the Highest Goal,
him I call a Brahmana.

The sun shines by day;
the moon is radiant by night.
The warrior king's armor shines.
In meditation, the Brahmana shines.
But all day and night
the Buddha shines in glory.

Because he has discarded evil,
he is called a Brahmana;
because he lives in peace,
he is called a Samana;
because he gives up the impurities,
he is called a Pabbajita - an ascetic.

One should not strike a Brahmana,
nor should a Brahmana vent his wrath
on one who has struck him.
Shame on him who strikes a Brahmana!
More shame on him
who gives vent to his wrath!

For Brahmana non-retaliation
is no small advantage.
When the mind is weaned
from things dear,
whenever the intent to harm ceases,
then and then only doth sorrow subside.

He who does no evil
through body, speech, or mind,

he who is retrained in these three respects,
him I call a Brahmana.

If from anybody one should understand
the Doctrine preached
by the Fully Enlightened One
that person should be devoutly revered,
as a Brahmana reveres
the sacrificial fire.

Not by matted hair,
nor by family,
nor by birth does
one become a Brahmana.
But the one in whom there exist
both truth and righteousness,
the pure one,
is a Brahmana .

What is the use of your matted hair,
O witless man?
What is the use of your
antelope skin garment?
Within, you are full of passions;
without, you embellish yourself.

The person who wears dust-heap robes,
who is lean,
whose veins stand out,
who meditates alone in the forest,
him I call a Brahmana.

The path of the Dhamma   **103**

I do not call him a Brahmana
merely because he is born of a Brahmin womb
or sprung from a Brahmin mother.
He is merely a ``Bhovadi'',
one addressed as ``Sir'',
if he is with attachments.
He who is free from attachments,
free from clinging -
him I call a Brahmana.

He who has cut off all chains,
who trembles not,
who has gone beyond ties,
who is unbound,
him I call a Brahmana.

He who has cut the strap of hatred,
the thong of craving,
and the rope of heresies,
together with the appendages of latent tendencies,
who has thrown up the cross-bar of ignorance,
who is an enlightened Buddha,
him I call a Brahmana.

He who, without anger,
endures reproach,
flogging and punishments,
whose power and the potent army is patience,
him I call a Brahmana.

The Dhammapada

He who is not wrathful,
but is dutiful, virtuous,
free from craving,
self-controlled and bears his final body,
him I call a Brahmana.

Like water on a lotus leaf,
like a mustard seed on the point of a needle,
he who clings not to sensual pleasures,
him I call a Brahmana.

He who realizes here in this world
the destruction of his sorrow,
who has laid the burden aside
and is emancipated,
him I call a Brahmana.

He whose knowledge is deep,
who is wise,
who is skilled in the right and wrong way,
who has reached the highest goal,
him I call a Brahmana.

He who is not intimate
either with householders
or with the homeless ones,
who wanders without an abode,
who is without desires,
him I call a Brahmana.

He who has laid aside the hammer
in his dealings with beings,
whether feeble or strong
who neither harms nor kills,
him I call a Brahmana.

He who is friendly amongst the hostile,
who is peaceful amongst the violent,
who is unattached amongst the attached,
him I call a Brahmana.

He who has overcome lust, hatred, pride,
detraction have fallen off like a mustard seed
from the point of a needle,
him I call a Brahmana.

He who utters gentle, instructive, true words,
who by his speech offends no one,
him I call a Brahmana.

He who in this world takes nothing
that is not given,
be it long or short, small or great, fair or foul,
him I call a Brahmana.

He who has no desires,
whether pertaining to this world
or to the next,
who is desireless and emancipated,
him I call a Brahmana.

He who has no longings,
who, through knowledge,
is free from doubts,
who has gained a firm footing
in the Deathless, Nibbana,
him I call a Brahmana.

He who has transcended
both good and bad
and the ties as well,
who is sorrowless, stainless, and pure,
him I call a Brahmana.

He who is spotless as the moon,
who is pure, serene, and unperturbed,
who has destroyed craving for becoming,
him I call a Brahmana.

He who has passed through this marsh,
this difficult path, the ocean of life, samsara,
and delusion, who has crossed and gone beyond,
who is meditative, free from craving and doubts,
who clinging to nothing,
has attained Nibbana,
him I call a Brahmana.

He who in this world giving up sensual desires,
would renounce worldly life
and become a homeless one,
he who has destroyed sensual desires

and continues to become,
him I call a Brahmana.

He who in this world giving up craving,
would renounce worldly life
and become a homeless one,
he who has destroyed craving and becoming,
him I call a Brahmana.

He who, discarding human ties
and transcending celestial ties,
is completely delivered from all ties,
him I call a Brahmana.

He who has given up likes and dislikes,
he who is cooled and is without flaw,
who has conquered the world,
and is devotional,
him I call a Brahmana.

He who in every way
knows the death and rebirth of beings,
who is non-attached,
well-gone, and enlightened,
him I call a Brahmana.

He whose destiny
neither gods nor Gandhabbas
nor men know,
who has destroyed all corruptions,

The Dhammapada

and is far removed from passions, Arahant,
him I call a Brahmana.

He who has no clinging to attachments
that are past, future, or present,
who is without clinging and grasping,
him I call a Brahmana.

The fearless, the noble, the hero,
the great sage, the conqueror, the desireless,
the cleanser of sin, the enlightened,
him I call a Brahmana.

That sage who knows his former dwellings,
who sees the blissful and the mournful states,
who has reached the end of births,
who, with superior wisdom,
has perfected himself,
who has completed the holy life,
and reached the end of all passions,
him I call a Brahmana.